A to Z China

BY JUSTINE AND RON FONTES

children's press

A Division of Scholastic Inc.
New York Toronto London Auckland Sydney
Mexico City New Delhi Hong Kong
Danbury, Connecticut

Series Consultant: Linda D. Bullock, Ph.D.
Series Design: Marie O'Neill
Photo Research: Candlepants Incorporated

The photos on the cover shows a bowl of chicken and vegetable ramen (top), the roof of the Forbidden City in Beijing (right), a young girl wearing traditional dress (bottom), and a Siberian Tiger (left).

In this book we use Ping Ying to phonetically spell out Chinese Words.

Fontes, Justine.
    China / by Justine and Ron Fontes.
            p. cm. – (A-Z)
Includes index. Audience: "Ages 7-9". Contents: Animals – Buildings – Cities – Dress – Exports – Food – Government – History – Important people – Jobs – Keepsakes– Land – Map – Nation – Only in China – People – Question – Religion – School and sports – Transportation – Unusual places – Visiting the country – Window to the past – X-tra special things – Yearly festivals – Zhalong – Let's explore more – Meet the authors – Chinese and english words.
    ISBN 0-516-24562-7 (lib. bdg.)   0-516-26807-4 (pbk.)
1. China–Juvenile literature. [1. China. 2. Alphabet.] I. Fontes, Ron. II. Title. III. Series.
    DS706.K67 2003
    [E] –dc21
                                    2003003702

1 2 3 4 5 6 7 8 9 10 R 12 11 10 09 08 07 06 05 04 03

■ Contents

Pandas

Animals

Yaks

Pandas, snow leopards, and golden monkeys live in China. There are also horses, camels, chickens, and pigs.

Snow leopard

Pandas spend at least 12 hours a day eating **bamboo**. Pandas have a bone in their front paws that works like an extra thumb. They use this thumb to push bamboo into their mouths.

Yaks live in China, too. A yak is an ox covered with thick, long, warm fur. Yaks are used for milk, meat, and fur. Before there were highways and farm machines, many Chinese people rode yaks to get around.

Families of golden monkeys live in trees.

Pagoda

Buildings

Chinese **emperors** and their families lived in the Forbidden City. They built huge, beautiful palaces with yellow roofs and red walls.

They also built pagodas. These are towers with roofs that turn up at the edges. Many Chinese believe pagodas bring wealth and happiness to the people who live near them.

Large cities in China have skyscrapers and other modern buildings. Hong Kong is one of the most modern cities in the world.

Hong Kong

Cities

■

Ch'eng

(Chun)
means city.

Millions of people live on the island of Hong Kong. Boats called junks and sampans float in the harbor. Beneath the water, a subway connects Hong Kong to the mainland. Hong Kong is famous for its busy life and tall buildings.

Another important city is Beijing, the capital of China. Many people visit to see the palaces of the Forbidden City. They also explore the temples, gardens, and parks there.

Shanghai is China's largest city and an important seaport. It is a center for trade and banking.

7

These people are practicing Tai Chi in modern clothing.

Dress

China has a long history. As times have changed, so have the clothes people wear.

This woman's dress is made of silk.

Silk is made from the cocoons of silk moths like this one.

Yi-fu

(YEE-foo)
means clothes.

The Chinese were the first people to make cloth from silk. Silk comes from the cocoons of moth caterpillars. Farmers send the cocoons to factories, where the threads are pulled apart and spun into silk threads.

Long ago, only rich people wore colorful silk clothing. Others wore clothes made from plant fibers, like banana leaves.

Miao children in traditional dress

These people are planting rice. China sells rice to Japan, Korea, and many other countries.

Exports

The best tea grows on steep cliffs. Monkeys are trained to climb the cliffs and pick the leaves.

The Chinese grow many crops to feed themselves and people around the world. They also export machines, cotton, clothing, tea, and toys.

Tea is one of China's major exports. In ancient times, traders traveled on camels across the deserts and mountains, carrying silk, tea, and other goods.

Chinese Egg Drop Soup Recipe

WHAT YOU NEED:
- 3 cups of chicken broth
- 1 green onion, chopped
- 2 eggs, slightly beaten
- pepper, garlic powder, or other spices you like

HOW TO MAKE IT:
Heat the broth to boiling in a medium saucepan. Add the onion. Then slowly add the beaten eggs to the boiling broth. Keep stirring. The soup is ready when the eggs are cooked.

Food

Soup is an important part of a Chinese meal.

Ask an adult to help you make egg drop soup using this recipe.

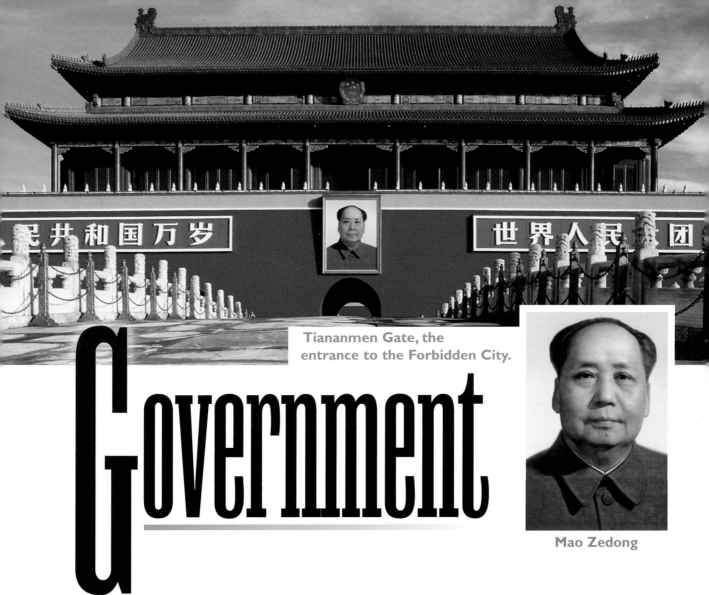

Tiananmen Gate, the entrance to the Forbidden City.

Mao Zedong

Government

Today, Jiang Zemin is the president of China.

Today, the Communist Party rules China. **Communism** is a system of government. Mao Zedong led the Communist Revolution and then ruled China from 1949 to 1976.

At age 18, people can vote for members of the National People's Congress. The president and members of the Congress serve for five years. One of their jobs is to carry out the orders of the leaders of the Communist Party.

Kuan Yin is the most popular goddess in China. This sculpture was made during the Qing Dynasty.

Confucius

History

There have been many Chinese dynasties. A dynasty is the name of a powerful family that ruled for many years. The Shang was China's first great dynasty. It began more than 4,000 years ago.

During each dynasty, many wonderful things were invented. Paper, eyeglasses, umbrellas, kites, gunpowder, fireworks, and the compass came from China. So did many of the world's greatest thinkers, including Confucius and Lao Tzu.

Important People

In Chinese art, an artist paints quickly to capture the spirit, or soul, of the subject.

Yishu-jia

(YEE-shu-jah)
means artist.

Zhang Lu painted *Waiting to Cross a River in Autumn* during the Ming Dynasty.

In the days of the dynasties, emperors paid artists to work. Many artists painted things from nature, like mountains, plants, and animals. They painted on rolls of paper or silk, using brushes and black ink made from **soot**. These artists painted what they saw with special brush strokes.

Jobs

Millions of people have left the countryside to find work in growing cities. Business is strong in China, but more than half of China's people are still farmers. Most farm in traditional ways, without tractors and other farm machines.

Fishing is also important in China. Some fish farmers raise fish in special ponds. Others catch fish the old-fashioned way. They tame wild water birds called **cormorants** to fish for them. These birds wear collars that won't let them swallow the fish.

Yumin means fisherman.

Most puppet shows tell folk stories.

Long ago, Chinese soldiers marched with kites. As the kites flew, wind whistled through bamboo pipes. The noise frightened their enemies.

Keepsakes

The Chinese have made kites for thousands of years. Even today, they fly kites made from bamboo and paper. You can buy kites in different shapes, such as birds, goldfish, butterflies, and dragons.

Puppets are also popular in China. There are many kinds of puppets such as hand or glove puppets and shadow puppets. Look for the **marionettes.** They have more than 40 strings each!

Rice Terraces

Land

Many of China's hillsides are carved into flat strips of land called terraces. These give farmers more soil in which to grow crops.

China has many mountains, including the Himalayas. Mt. Everest, the highest mountain in the world, sits on China's southern border.

Two of the world's longest rivers flow through China. They are the Huang He, or Yellow River, and the Yangtze.

The Yangtze River divides the north from the south. Many people live on the land around the Yangtze because the soil is rich and gets lots of rain.

Large deserts, like the Gobi Desert, cover much of western China. Southern China is warm and has many waterfalls.

Jiang

(jung)
means river.

19

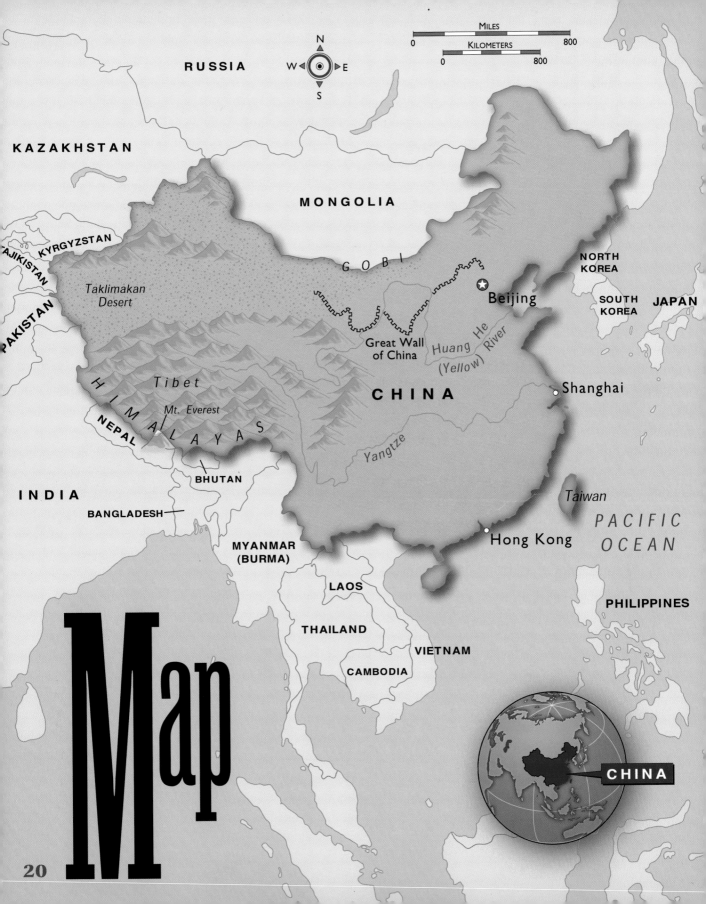

RUSSIA

KAZAKHSTAN

TAJIKISTAN

KYRGYZSTAN

PAKISTAN

MONGOLIA

G O B I

Taklimakan
Desert

Great Wall
of China

Beijing

NORTH
KOREA

SOUTH
KOREA

JAPAN

Huang He
(Yellow) River

CHINA

Shanghai

T i b e t

HIMALAYAS

Mt. Everest

NEPAL

BHUTAN

Yangtze

Taiwan

PACIFIC
OCEAN

INDIA

BANGLADESH

MYANMAR
(BURMA)

Hong Kong

LAOS

PHILIPPINES

THAILAND

VIETNAM

CAMBODIA

Map

CHINA

Nation

Qi

(chee)
means flag.

China's flag is red with five yellow stars. The red stands for the Communist Revolution that changed China's government. The large yellow star stands for the Communist Party, the people who rule China. The four small stars stand for the Chinese people brought together by the Party.

President Mao Zedong raised this flag for the first time on October 1, 1949, over Tiananmen Square in Beijing. Each day, as the sun rises, China's flag goes up over the square.

Only in China

Colorful operas mix music, **pantomime**, dance, **acrobatics**, and song.

Actors in Chinese Opera wear colorful costumes and make-up.

The stage is often bare. The actors do not use props. Instead, they perform special actions to tell a story. For example, walking in a circle means taking a long journey. Drummers drum while actors move and sing.

These operas last a long time. Families may spend hours watching. They may even sing along.

Geju

(JING-shee)
means opera.

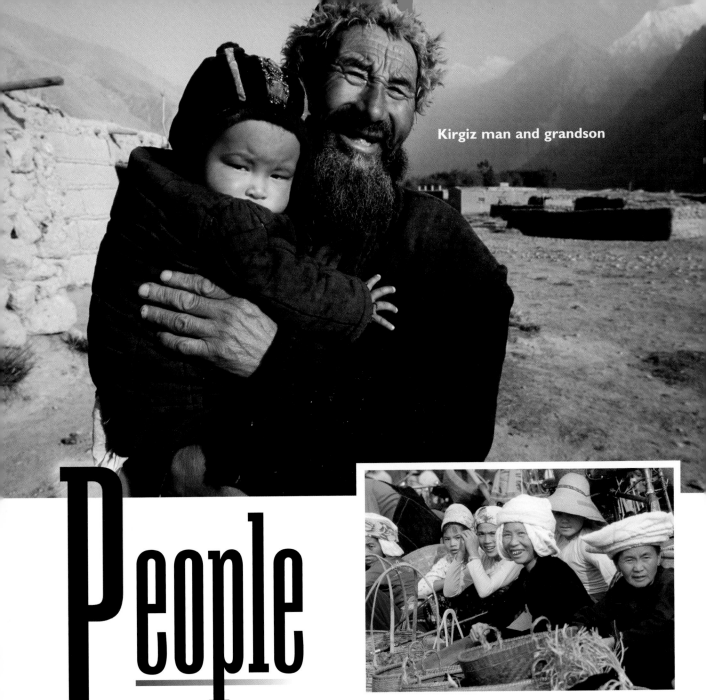

Kirgiz man and grandson

People

There are more than one billion people in China. That is more than any other country in the world.

Some people live in yurts. They are round tents made from animal hides or felt.

Ren

means
people.

Most Chinese are Hans. Han people have dark hair and almond-shaped eyes. They speak some form of Chinese.

There are also 55 smaller groups of people. Most of these people speak and write Chinese, too. They also have their own languages and alphabets.

Most people live along its crowded coast. The cities are crowded too. People live and work close together.

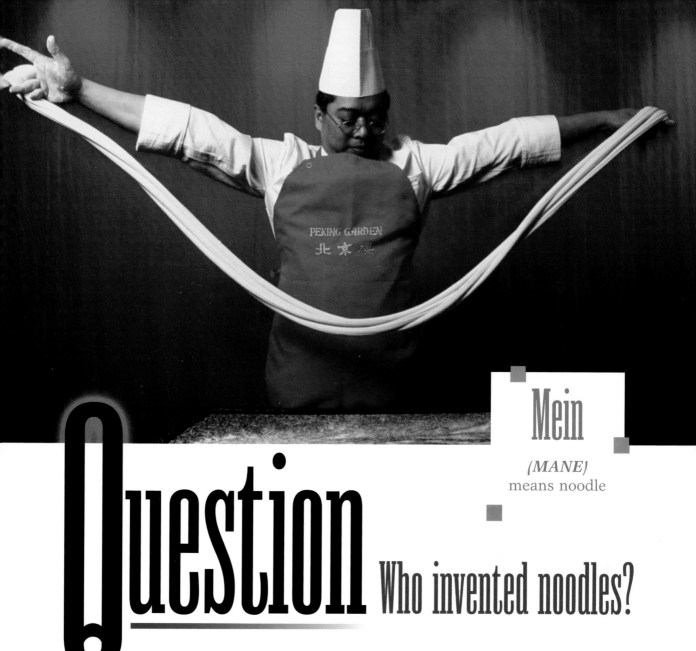

Question Who invented noodles?

Mein

(MANE) means noodle

When you visit an Italian restaurant, do you like to order spaghetti and meatballs? You might have thought the noodles came from Italy, but they don't. The Italian explorer Marco Polo brought noodles to Italy in the 1300s. He brought them from his travels in China, where noodles were invented more than 5,000 years ago.

Each part of China has its own special noodles. Long noodles mean long life, so Chinese people eat noodles to celebrate birthdays.

The lotus flower is a Buddhist symbol of happiness.

Tibetan prayer wheel

Dalai Lama

Religion

In China, the three religions with the most followers are Buddhism, Taoism, and Confucianism. There are very few Muslims and Christians.

Buddhism teaches peace and happiness through self-control. In Taoism, followers live a simple life close to nature. Confucianism is based on the writings of a wise man named Confucius. These three religions show a love of nature.

Almost all of the people in Tibet, in southwestern China, are Buddhists. Their leader is called the Dalai Lama.

27

School & Sports

Children begin school at age six and one-half. They learn reading, writing, math, and other subjects. It takes a long time for children to learn to read and write Chinese. That is because the language has more than 50,000 characters.

Many athletes become great acrobats, who tumble and do tricks in the air. Some sports that began in China include rowing, tug-of-war, and **martial arts**. Today, Chinese athletes win many world championships.

Transportation

City streets are crowded with people riding on bicycles. Buses carry people where they want to go more often than cars. Cars are expensive, but more people are beginning to drive. Air pollution is a problem in China.

There are many miles of railroad tracks across China. The trains used to run on steam. Today, most trains run on electricity.

People travel by water, too. Harbors are filled with small boats and large ships. Boats on the Yangtze River take people to some of China's biggest cities.

Unusual Places

Qin Shihuangdi was the first emperor of China. He helped bring China's many different people together. The Qin dynasty ended after the emperor died.

Thousands of workers were forced to build the emperor's tomb. Inside the tomb, there are horses made from clay and wooden chariots. There is also an army of 6,000 soldiers made from clay. The soldiers are life-sized, and no two look alike. The emperor thought the soldiers would protect him in the afterlife.

30

The Great Wall of China is so big that astronauts can see its shadow from space.

Visiting the Country

Before the Qin Dynasty, China had many kingdoms. Kings built walls around their land. Together, the pieces formed the Great Wall.

Over time, thousands of workers were forced to help build the wall. Today, the wall is more than 4,000 miles (6,437 km) long. It is the largest structure ever built. Six tall men would have to stand on top of each other to reach the tallest part of the wall.

Window to the Past

When an emperor died, his oldest son took over. Sometimes the new emperor was only a child when he took the throne.

This boy emperor, Kuang Hsu, had no real power, but he had many servants.

In the past, many Chinese people carried passengers in rickshaws, or hand-pulled carts. Today, many people ride in taxis.

When emperors ruled, all people had a certain place in **society**. Some people had high rank. Others had no rank at all. When people saw someone with higher rank, they were expected to **kowtow**. They bowed three times and touched their noses to the floor.

Leshan Buddha

X-tra Special Things

Mahjong

Chinese acrobat

Students need to know about 6,000 symbols to read a newspaper.

Shu fa

(SHOO-fah) means writing.

The Chinese are famous for doing many things.

Chinese acrobats are some of the finest in the world. Jackie Chan, a movie star, trained as an acrobat.

The Chinese carved the giant Leshan Buddha into a cliff where three rivers meet. It is the largest stone **sculpture** in the world.

They also invented mahjong, a game played with 136 tiles.

Dances and a Great Prayer Festival are part of the Tibetan New Year celebration.

Yearly Festivals

The celebration for Chinese New Year lasts two weeks. The Lantern Festival ends the holiday.

New Year's Lantern Festival

Costumed performers prepare for the Lion Dance.

The Chinese use a **lunar** calendar, which follows the moon. Their New Year begins at the end of January. The party begins with loud drums, gongs, and lion dances. People celebrate the holiday feasting with their families.

The spring brings the Clear and Bright Festival. People have picnics at the cemetery to pay respect to their dead **ancestors**.

In the Mid-Autumn Festival, families celebrate the moon. They eat sweet mooncakes and light paper lanterns.

Cranes dance in pairs or flocks.

Zhalong

Shengming
means life.

Almost 200 different kinds of birds stop to rest and lay eggs in Zhalong each year.

Zhalong is a nature reserve. The land and birds are protected. People watch for cranes, graceful birds with long necks. There are different kinds of cranes. The red-crowned crane is especially important. The Chinese enjoy and respect cranes very much. This bird is a symbol of long life.

■ Chinese and English Words

acrobat (AK-ruh-bat) a person trained to perform athletic tricks

ancestor (AN-sess-tur) family members who lived long ago, usually before grandparents

bamboo a kind of giant, woody grass

ch'eng (chun) Chinese word for city

communism (CAWM-yuh-ni-zuhm) a system of government in which all property is shared

cormorant (KAW-muh-rant) a black, sea bird that dives for fish

dong-wu Chinese word for animal

emperor (EM-puhr-uhr) the leader of an Empire, which is a group of lands or countries

geju (JING-shee) Chinese word for opera

harbor (HAR-bur) a place where ships stop to load or unload cargo

jiang (jung) Chinese word for river

lunar (LOO-nur) having to do with the moon

marionette (mar-ee-uh-NET) a puppet that is moved by pulling strings

martial art (mar-SHUHL art) fighting sports like judo and karate developed to make self defense possible without weapons

mein (mane) Chinese word for noodles

palace (PAL-iss) a home for a king, queen, or other rulers

qi (chee) Chinese word for flag

ren Chinese word for people

revolution (rev-uh-LOO-shuhn) a change of government brought about by force; sometimes used to mean any big change

sculpture (SKUHLP-chur) something shaped out of wood, stone, clay or other materials

shufa (SHOO-fah) Chinese word for calligraphy or writing

soot (sut) the result of burning coal, wood, or oil

yi-fu (YEE-fu) Chinese word for clothes

yishu-jia (YEE-shu-jah) Chinese word for artist

yumin Chinese word for fisherman

■ Let's Explore More

MOONBEAMS, DUMPLINGS & DRAGON BOATS A Treasury of Chinese Holiday Tales, Activities and Recipes by Nina Simonds, Leslie Swartz, and The Children's Museum, Boston, Gulliver Books, 2002

LOOK WHAT CAME FROM CHINA by Miles Harvey, Franklin Watts, 1998

Websites

http://library.thinkquest.org/26469/
Learn about China and take fun quizzes on this site created by kids for kids.

www.atozkidsstuff.com/china.html
You'll find Chinese history, places, photos and more.

www.gigglepotz.com/china.htm
Get a Chinese name, write Chinese characters, learn about dragons and making silk, and other fun things.

Italic page numbers indicate illustrations.

Meet the Authors

JUSTINE & RON FONTES have written nearly 400 children's books together. Since 1988, they have published *critter news*, a free newsletter that keeps them in touch with publishers from their home in Maine.

The Fonteses have written many biographies and early readers, as well as historical novels and other books combining facts with stories. Their love of animals is expressed in the nature notes columns of *critter news*.

During his childhood in Tennessee, Ron was a member of the Junior Classical League and went on to tutor Latin students. At 16, Ron was drawing a science fiction comic strip for the local newspaper. A professional artist for 30 years, Ron has also been in theater as a costumer, makeup artist, and designer.

Justine was born in New York City and worked in publishing while earning a BA in English Literature Phi Beta Kappa from New York University. Thanks to her parents' love of travel, Justine visited most of Europe as a child, going as far north as Finland. During college, she spent time in France and Spain.